NATIONAL
GEOGRAPHIC

T0042333

Freedom Readers

PATHFINDER EDITION

By Fran Downey

CONTENTS

Freedom
Readers

~~~~~~~~~~ ◆◆◆ ~~~~~~~~~~

What does reading mean to you? For African American slaves, it meant freedom.

~~~~~~~~~~ ◆◆◆ ~~~~~~~~~~

By Fran Downey

You can read whenever you want to, but that has not always been true for everyone in the United States. Some people in the past had to struggle for the freedom to read.

Long ago, slave owners did not let slaves learn to read. They were afraid that if slaves could read, they would want freedom. Many owners punished slaves who were caught with books or caught trying to learn to read.

Still, many slaves did learn to read. They knew that reading was important and that reading would help them gain freedom. Let's meet some of these freedom readers.

A Chief's Son

Olaudah Equiano

◆ ◆ ◆

Olaudah Equiano was born in Africa in 1745, and his father was a chief. Young Equiano had lots of free time, so he spent most of his time playing.

One day, he was playing with his sister when a group of strangers surprised and **kidnapped** them. Both brother and sister were marched to the coast. Equiano was about ten years old at the time.

A naval officer bought Equiano, and he was taken aboard a ship. He was forced to work as the naval officer's servant.

Aboard ship, Equiano saw many strange things. One of them was books. He saw his master and other people reading books. However, he could not figure out what they were doing with the books. He knew his master learned from books, but he didn't know how he did it.

Equiano tried everything he could think of. He held books to his ears, but they were quiet. He even asked books questions, but that did not work either because the books did not speak to him.

Later, Equiano found out that books do not talk. Friends taught him to read and write. After growing up, Equiano spent some of his free time working, and he earned enough money to buy his freedom. He moved to England, and there he wrote a book about his life. It explained to people that slavery was evil. Through his book, Equiano worked to **abolish,** or end, slavery.

Olaudah Equiano

Freedom Lost. *An American slave ship sails off the coast of Africa.*

The Poet
Phillis Wheatley

◆ ◆ ◆

Slave Sale. *Men, women, and children were sold at auctions like the one pictured.*

Phillis Wheatley

Phillis Wheatley was born in Africa in about 1753. She was also kidnapped and sold into slavery. She did not know what would happen next. Her captors took her from Africa to Boston, Massachusetts, where she was sold at a slave auction to a man named John Wheatley. Phyllis was just seven years old.

The Wheatley family wanted the young slave to work in their home as their servant, but that soon changed. The Wheatleys raised her with their two children, and they treated her as if she were one of their daughters. They taught her many things and she thrived.

Wheatley was very smart. One of the other children taught her to read and write English, and by the time she was 12, Wheatley could also read and write Greek and Latin. Neighbors soon learned about this smart girl.

When she was 13, Wheatley wrote her first poem. She went on to write many more. In 1773, she became the first African American woman to write a book. It had 39 poems.

During the American Revolution, Wheatley wrote poems about freedom, and she even met George Washington. She also wrote that slavery should end.

Freedom Fighter
Frederick Douglass

◆ ◆ ◆

CAROL M. HIGHSMITH/BUYENLARGE/GETTY IMAGES (ART); © STOCK MONTAGE/ALAMY (PORTRAIT)

Frederick Douglass

Free at Last. *An artist shows President Abraham Lincoln meeting Frederick Douglass.*

Frederick Douglass was born into slavery in about 1818. He was born on a **plantation,** or large farm, in Maryland. When he was six years old, Douglass was taken to another plantation.

A few years later, Douglass was taken to Baltimore. Life in the city was different than on a plantation. He had to run errands and take care of his master's young son.

Douglass asked his master's wife to teach him to read and she agreed. He quickly learned the alphabet and wanted to learn more.

But things changed when Douglass's master found out. He stopped the lessons.

Young Douglass then learned to read in secret. He tricked children into teaching him to read. He read newspapers at home, but his master yelled whenever he caught Douglass reading.

Douglass kept on reading, and he also learned to write. He then ran away from his master. He boarded a train and moved to the North, where slavery was illegal.

This is just the beginning of Douglass's amazing story. He spent many years fighting slavery. He started a newspaper, which was called the *North Star.* He also wrote several books, and he even met President Abraham Lincoln. His efforts helped end slavery in 1865.

More Freedom Readers

❖ ❖ ❖

So far, you've met three African American slaves who learned to read. But they were not the only ones. Many others also learned to read, and they risked their lives to do so.

No one knows exactly how many slaves learned to read because most of them kept the skill a secret. They were afraid of being punished.

Lucius Holsey owned five books, two of which were spelling books. One by one, he learned all the words in the spelling books.

Thomas Jones also learned to read from a spelling book. He paid another child six cents a week to teach him to spell. The child taught him words that had one and two **syllables.** After that, Thomas taught himself new words.

Not all slaves had spelling books. Some had to learn to read in other ways. A slave who lived in Georgia learned to spell before he could read. He heard people spell words out loud, and he repeated what he heard. Then he read street signs and store signs. Many other slaves also used signs to learn to spell.

Many slaves learned to read because they wanted freedom. Take Sella Martin, for instance. He wanted to run away from slavery. He spelled words he saw on signs. News quickly spread that Martin could read.

One night a group of slaves showed up at the hotel where Martin worked. Each had stolen a book or newspaper for Martin because they all wanted to help him learn to read.

The Civil War ended slavery in 1865, so many former slaves were allowed to go to school. They knew that reading would help them live as free people.

Wordwise

abolish: to end

kidnap: to steal a person

plantation: large farm

syllable: part of a word

On the Run. *Some slaves fled to the North in search of freedom.*

From Slavery

Hard Work. *After the Civil War, many former slaves worked on other people's farms because they didn't have land of their own.*

to Freedom

Slaves were denied an education. But that wasn't all. They weren't allowed to own land. They couldn't vote. They couldn't even get married legally. According to the law, they were property. They had no rights. Slaves were workers. That was all.

Most slaves worked on plantations, or large southern farms. They worked long hours in the fields. They tended and harvested crops, such as tobacco and cotton.

Farm Work

After the Civil War, slavery was officially outlawed in the United States, and nearly four million slaves were freed. For the first time, they were allowed to choose where they worked and what they did.

Yet many former slaves stayed in the same place and kept farming, even though it was hard work. Some even farmed land for their former masters. Why?

Former slaves still had few choices about the work they did. They had little or no education, so that meant they could not get other kinds of jobs. They also did not have money to buy homes or land of their own.

For African Americans, true freedom was still a long way off. Many barriers still stood in their way.

Finding Freedom

Education was one of the keys to freedom. Only when former slaves learned to read and write would they have access to new kinds of jobs.

Some African Americans were able to attend schools with teachers. That was the case in Savannah, Georgia. About 500 African American students attended school there. The schools didn't have vacations. But the students didn't want them because they just wanted to learn.

Other African Americans still could not go to school, so sometimes they learned to read in churches or from friends.

Years of Progress

Getting an education was an important step toward equality. Yet getting the rights of other Americans took time. For example, even though slaves were now free, they still weren't American citizens. They had to wait until 1868 for that. They couldn't vote until 1870.

With each victory, African Americans gained more power to shape the future. They began to serve in state and federal governments. Between 1870 and 1890, more than 20 African Americans served as members of Congress. They played important roles in rebuilding a country broken apart by war.

Attending School. *For African Americans, getting an education was one way to become truly free.*

The Costs of Freedom

Former slaves faced challenges long after the Civil War ended. For one thing, there weren't enough schools. Many children also had to work to help their families survive, so getting an education was not always an option.

Land and money were big problems, too. In the South, many former slaves had to rent homes and farmland from whites. Most of their money went toward rent. They also had to pay for food and clothes.

Farmers had other costs, too. They needed seeds and farm equipment. They also had to buy farm animals and feed. It was hard to get ahead after all these costs.

Free But Not Equal

Former slaves had won their freedom, but their hardships were not over. They soon learned that equality is about more than just freedom. It's about equal opportunities and equal education. It's about equal pay and equal rights. It's also about being treated as equals.

After the Civil War, many people continued to treat African Americans like they were slaves. Only in the 1960s, when the Civil Rights Movement began, did the hope of true equality return. That's when people hoped again that African Americans would one day have the same rights as other Americans.

Growing Problems. *Farming was expensive. Former slaves had to pay for land, animals, seeds, and tools.*

Finding Freedom

Read on to see what you learned about slavery and freedom.

1 Why did slaves want to learn how to read?

2 Who was Frederick Douglass? Why is he famous?

3 What are some of the ways African Americans learned how to read?

4 After slavery ended, how was life different for African Americans?

5 Why did African Americans still have many hardships after the Civil War?